For Raman & C

   A true del
in celebrating the beautiful union
of two people we dearly love.
I look forward to when our
paths cross again. Best
wishes to you and your family!
                              Nija

   August '09

The GROUP

An Amazing Way to Achieve Success, Happiness & Extraordinary Relationships

REBECCA CARSWELL   MIRJA HEIDE   TIFFANY KAHARICK   AMY MEAD

DC PRESS

A Division of the Diogenes Consortium
SANFORD • FLORIDA

© 2009 Rebecca Carswell, Mirja Heide, Tiffany Kaharick & Amy Mead

All rights reserved. No part of this manuscript may be reproduced or transmitted in any form or by any means, electronic or mechanical, including photocopying, recording, or any information storage and retrieval system, without permission in writing from DC Press.

Published by DC Press
2445 River Tree Circle
Sanford, FL 32771
http://www.focusonethics.com

For orders other than individual consumers, DC Press grants discounts on purchases of 10 or more copies of single titles for bulk use, special markets, or premium use. For further details, contact:
Special Sales — DC Press
2445 River Tree Circle, Sanford, FL 32771
TEL: 866-602-1476

Book set in: Adobe Minion Pro
Cover Design and Composition: Jonathan Pennell & Amy Mead
Photographer: Diane Dultmeier

Library of Congress Catalog Number: 2009924871
   Carswell. Rebecca, Heide. Mirja, Kaharick. Tiffany, and Mead. Amy
The GROUP: An Amazing Way to Achieve Success, Happiness & Extraordinary Relationships
   ISBN: 978-1-932021-38-7

First DC Press Edition
10 9 8 7 6 5 4 3 2 1

Printed in the United States of America

Throughout the centuries, people have gathered in groups to grow, prosper and exchange ideas, laying the foundation for universal and timeless concepts. The authors do not claim any credit for the idea of meeting in groups, as it is not a new concept. They simply wish to share the particular process that they have created and found to result in great success and happiness in their own lives.

Contents

Foreword 7

Infinite Possibilities Await You 11

Our Success Stories 13

Chapter 1:
Understanding the Power of The GROUP 15

Chapter 2:
Manifesting: Transforming Your Dreams into Reality 21
    Imagination 27
    Clarity 34
    Belief 40
    Flexibility 46
    Trust 52
    Action 60

Chapter 3:
Creating The Ideal GROUP Atmosphere 67

Chapter 4:
Active Listening: The Key to Understanding Others 89

Chapter 5:
The Structure of The GROUP Meeting   95
    Outline of The GROUP Meeting   114

Chapter 6:
The Roles of The GROUP Meeting   117
    Checklist for Each Meeting   135

Chapter 7:
How to Form The GROUP   139
    First Meeting   150

Chapter 8:
Permission to Dream   153

Chapter 9:
Living Your Dreams   155

Our Offerings from The GROUP Meetings   157

Notes   165

Author Biographies   167

To Reach the Authors   171

Foreword

by Dr. Lewis Losoncy

The GROUP may very well prove to be the most important and practical book on how to transform ordinary relationships into extraordinary ones. This brilliant idea was developed by four Florida friends: Rebecca Carswell, Mirja Heide, Tiffany Kaharick and Amy Mead. Their discovery: the way to manifest one's individual dreams is through the power of exceptional relationships. The four authors designed a safe, supportive, respectful and encouraging atmosphere to bring out the best in each other.

The GROUP time together becomes that special two hours a month where, in this positive atmosphere, each member gains strength to face life's challenges and climb life's mountains. They share their anxieties and fears as well as their dreams during these moments. And then, through the collective warmth, wit and wisdom of The GROUP, each chooses courage over discouragement.

As a psychotherapist, I was fascinated with how the authors built The GROUP consistent with sound motivational and relationship principles, without bogging the reader down with theory. Alfred Adler's ideas on the importance of social-connectedness and encouragement, Carl Rogers' *Person-Centering*, and Martin Seligman's *Positive Psychology* would buy into the ideas of The GROUP. Yet, no knowledge of psychology is a prerequisite to turn a group into The GROUP.

After the astounding success of The GROUP, the four authors took this powerful growth process to others: in the workplace, homes, teams and organizations. Soon others started realizing their dreams *and* experiencing equally exhilarating feelings by finding their autograph on the growth and success of others. Yet it is not surprising about the synergistic effect of a manifesting group like The GROUP. Mark Twain called synergy, "the bonus that is achieved when things work together harmoniously." Why? A group of four individuals has an *additive* power, $1 + 1 + 1 + 1 = 4$. The GROUP's synergy of four people has a *multiplicative* power, $1 \times 2 \times 3 \times 4 = 24$!

Two other appeals of The GROUP process are its simplicity and its practicality. Easy and doable! The authors streamlined the process for the reader, and for each member invited to become part of the experience. Reading The GROUP is the only requirement to understand, become motivated and inspired, and to give and get the benefits of this magical process of group manifesting.

There is a huge difference between a group and The GROUP. A group in the workplace has gripe sessions. In The GROUP, in the same workplace with the same people, gripe sessions are transformed into growth sessions. The GROUP in a family becomes a place where children learn they can be encouragers to their parents, and parents' eyes open to their children's dreams. When sports teams use The GROUP method, they gain respect for teammates and a desire to cooperate, rather than to compete, for one shared dream. The GROUP, from settings in education and business to church and families, helps people empathize, understand, appreciate and encourage each other en route to their dreams.

The GROUP has the power to lift all of your relationships higher. As you move through these pages you come to life again. You will be excited about sharing these ideas with others and getting your own GROUP started. And those with whom you share the book will sign on, thanking you for your discovery.

The GROUP is the book you have been waiting for to change your life. Here it is. Thanks Rebecca, Mirja, Tiffany and Amy. You started something to give to each other, and discovered something to give to the world!

—**Dr. Lewis Losoncy**, Psychotherapist
Author of *If It Weren't For You, We Could Get Along: How to Stop Blaming and Start Living*

Infinite Possibilities Await You

"A journey of a thousand miles begins
with a single step."

—Lao Tzu

When a train pulls out of the station it is a little sluggish, straining slightly to gain speed. The turning of the wheels and gears has no rhythm yet. But as the train accelerates, the rhythm begins to build. Once it is moving, it takes a lot to stop it. The train has momentum, energy and incredible power behind it!

The GROUP is like this train. The collective energy of The GROUP creates momentum. As you hold your meetings you notice a synergy, a powerful force that is exponentially stronger than that of the individual. The degree to which you can focus on your dreams and goals improves. As your dreams and goals take physical form, the belief in your own abilities and those of others grows. Your GROUP evolves and reveals just how powerful all of you are...individually and collectively. You support others in their success while being encouraged and supported yourself. You break down old barriers and lay down new tracks. Changes take place in your life and in the lives of everyone in your GROUP.

As our lives changed in positive ways because of The GROUP, we began talking about what the world would be like if more people had the inspiration and encouragement we were experiencing. We imagined people supporting each other the way we have, and lives changing for the better. This vision of a better world grew into the desire to help others benefit from what we have learned.

We are four women who wanted to add magic to our lives. We wanted our lives to be *extraordinary*. We had no idea what we would discover by forming The GROUP. We discovered, just as you will, that we are unlimited in what we can accomplish. We can dream and achieve what we never before thought possible. We are meant to live the lives we dream of living.

Climb aboard this train and take a journey with us. Let this book guide you to your own discoveries. An extraordinary adventure of infinite possibilities awaits you!

Our Success Stories

One of the many rewards of being part of The GROUP is celebrating success. The following stories are from our own lives. It is our successes that continue to inspire us and remind us of what we can accomplish.

    A Sailing Adventure   22
    Dreaming of Africa   42
    Manifesting a Luxury Car   47
    Anything is Possible   53
    Our Dream Home   62
    A Simple Gift   102
    Overnight Success   105
    I'm Pregnant!   112

1
Understanding the Power of The GROUP

"I have always had close friends. But what takes place with The GROUP is different. The strength of multiple minds, the power of the combined energy, a group of people who believe in you...there's nothing like it."

— AMY MEAD

Something interesting happens when you state what you want out loud in front of people who believe in you and support you in achieving your goals. You start believing, too. *Believing* you can have what you want is an important aspect of *creating* what you want. When you surround yourself with supportive people who encourage you to dream and remind you that anything is possible, believing and creating become easier. Other people are not aware of the limitations you may place on yourself from past experiences or setbacks. Others see you more objectively. They see the whole you. They believe in you — sometimes even more than you believe in yourself.

What makes The GROUP so powerful?

Fresh Ideas, Different Perspectives

At times you may not see the full range of possibilities that exists when seeking to accomplish your goals. By being part of The GROUP, you tap into the power of multiple minds. You draw on the ideas, wisdom and experience of every person in The GROUP. They help illuminate answers that lie within you and guide you to solutions. They help you see things from different perspectives, opening your eyes to new ways of accomplishing your goals. What may not have seemed possible in the past is now within reach.

Understanding the Power of The GROUP 17

Support

Being part of The GROUP helps you let go of the belief that you have to accomplish everything on your own. You recognize that you are supported. Your GROUP is rooting for you, not only during each meeting, but also in the days and weeks between the meetings.

A Plan of Action

You leave your GROUP meeting with a written plan of action, ideas and tools to achieve your goals. You are ready to move forward and you know how to do so.

Accountability

When you discuss specific action steps with your GROUP, you are inspired to follow through and take action. Your GROUP brings accountability into your life as it takes you from talking about your dreams to achieving your dreams. Regular meetings keep you motivated to continue manifesting your goals.

Empowerment

It is rewarding to be celebrated when you accomplish a goal. You also listen to others express their goals and then celebrate when those goals are accomplished. When you share in the excitement of watching others turn possibility into reality, you are empowered. When one person wins, everyone wins.

Trust

Words spoken during your meetings are private and should never go outside of The GROUP. Honor, trust and privilege are an important part of The GROUP. It is an honor to be present when others share something personal. It is an act of trust on their part. For the listener, it is a privilege to be trusted in this way.

Combined Energy

When a group of people come together a powerful energy is formed...an energy that is greater than that of the individual. When the combined energy from

Understanding the Power of The GROUP 19

your GROUP is directed toward you, you are more likely to make changes and accomplish your goals. Dreams are revealed. Discoveries are made. You witness a powerful change in others and in yourself. You help and support others, and by helping others, you help yourself. You accomplish your dreams and help others do the same. You believe in yourself and see that same belief grow in others. You feel recharged, empowered and ready to take action. The GROUP allows you to share in the experience of understanding and being understood, supporting and being supported and creating the life you want.

2
Manifesting: Transforming Your Dreams into Reality

> "The greatest achievement was at first and for a time a dream. The oak sleeps in the acorn; the bird waits in the egg. Dreams are the seedlings of realities."
>
> — James Allen

Manifesting is designing each day by setting an intention for what you want and then moving in the direction of that intention. You think about it, believe you can have it, focus your energy on it, and you act in the direction of that desire. Then the shift begins to happen.

To manifest is to take action…on a physical level, a mental level and an emotional level.

Manifesting begins with a thought. That thought inspires an idea. What will you do with that idea? Manifesting involves making a choice to believe in that idea. If you believe in the idea, you cultivate it. You think about it. You write down your thoughts. You dream. You visualize. You imagine what your life will be like when that idea becomes reality. You start moving in the direction of the idea in the physical realm. You make choices that will support the idea... stepping stones that lead you to your dreams.

The following story illustrates how Amy, one of the authors, manifested her dream of living on a sailboat:

A Sailing Adventure

My boyfriend and I were living in one of Chicago's most beautiful suburbs. We lived in a fantastic house on 20 acres of land that overlooked two lakes. We both had good jobs and a wonderful lifestyle. By all outward accounts, we had a great life. But there was one problem: I was unhappy. I had a long commute, was completely burned out at my job and was sick of the bitter cold Chicago winters. I felt like I was on a treadmill to a nervous breakdown. I wanted to start over and do something completely different.

My boyfriend and I began dreaming about a radical change in our lives — the possibility of owning and living on a sailboat.

In spite of demanding jobs and limited time, we spent the next six months imagining and talking about what it would be like to follow this dream. We were single-minded in our purpose. We spent countless hours on the Internet at night looking at sailboats. We knew nothing about them or even which one would be right for us. We didn't know how we were going to pull the whole thing off. However, we were so focused, so intent and so immersed in our goal that we made it happen.

Despite some fear and trepidation, we quit our jobs, put everything in storage, and left Chicago. On December 7, we moved to Florida and on December 14 we bought a small 27-foot sailboat. We spent six months working non-stop to convert our sailboat into a vessel that we could live on. This was quite a feat considering that neither of us was the slightest bit handy or knew anything whatsoever about boats or sailing.

The first sail that we undertook was crossing the Gulf Stream (one of the most potentially treacherous crossings there is) in the middle of the night from Miami to the Bahamas. We were doing it! We were living our dream!

We spent one year living on our tiny boat, three months of which were spent in the Bahamas. We learned to spear fish, navigate and survive at sea and at anchor. We also weathered some horrendous storms. Emotionally, we experienced some of the most intense highs and lows we had ever felt in our lives — from utter elation to absolute fear, and everything in between. Our sailing trip was the greatest adventure we've had in our lives.

When we started The GROUP five years later, I learned what manifesting is and how it works. It was only then that I realized I had already manifested the greatest adventure of my life. The combination of talking and dreaming about it, taking action and believing we could do it made it all happen.

Now, thanks to The GROUP, I have an even greater awareness of what manifesting is. I have more tools and more support, which has made me even better at creating what I want in my life.

Climb outside of any limitations you may have placed on yourself and dream big. You may want to manifest something tangible such as more money, a relationship, or a new job. Or you may want to change how you feel such as improving your self-esteem, creating more joy and happiness, or practicing forgiveness. You can just as easily create a particular state of being as you can a material possession.

Six important components will help you transform your dreams into reality:

- Imagination
- Clarity
- Belief
- Flexibility
- Trust
- Action

Imagination

"Imagination is more important than knowledge. For while knowledge defines all we currently know and understand, imagination points to all we might yet discover and create."

—Albert Einstein

If you could have anything you desired in your life, what would that be? Imagine the life you wish to live and the people and things you wish to have in your life.

Imagination takes what begins as a thought and transforms it into something more tangible. All great creations began as a thought in someone's mind.

Hold a thought or an image of what you want in your mind for a moment. As you do this, add details. How do you see yourself? How will you feel when you have achieved your goal? Describe any emotions you experience. What will your life be like when your dream is a reality?

Do you remember how you imagined as a child? Children possess vivid imaginations, unhindered by limiting thoughts or beliefs. Children do not harbor such thoughts as 'I can't,' 'that's not realistic,' 'that's not practical' or 'that's impossible.' In children, imagination and creativity exist in their truest and purest form. Tap into this innate ability and let your imagination run wild. Imagination and belief go hand in hand, and both are paramount to manifesting.

We are born with the ability to use our imagination to an unlimited degree. Perhaps over time our imagination has taken a back seat to the practical aspects of life. We adopt — often unknowingly — the beliefs of family, friends, spouses, and society. Try to set aside any limiting beliefs you may have adopted from others and give yourself permission to imagine freely.

You can tap back into your imagination any time. Try the exercise below to see how easy it is to reignite your imagination. If possible, have someone slowly read the following out loud to you:

> *Close your eyes. Imagine, sense or feel that you are standing in your kitchen, barefoot. Notice how the kitchen floor feels beneath your feet. Is it tile, wood, carpet, a rug? Notice how it feels.*
>
> *Now notice your kitchen. Notice the placement of your kitchen cabinets — what they look like... the color...the texture. Notice your refrigerator — where it is located...its color...what it looks like. Imagine, sense or feel that you walk over to your refrigerator and open it up. Notice what the handle feels like in your hand as you open the door.*

Imagine that in the center of your refrigerator is a perfectly ripe lemon. Take the lemon out and hold it in your hand. Notice how it feels in your hand. Imagine the lemon...the rough texture...the bumpy, oily little dimples...the funny nubs on each end...perhaps those nubs are slightly greenish in color.

Now imagine that you take the lemon over to a counter top or chopping board. Imagine that you pick up a knife and cut the lemon in half. Perhaps you cut through a few seeds and as you cut the lemon, juice squirts.

Imagine, sense or feel that you bring half of the lemon up to your face, to your nose. Take a deep breath in through your nose and smell the lemon. Notice the fresh scent.

Now imagine that you lower the lemon just a little to your mouth. Take a nice, big bite out of the lemon. Notice what happens. Perhaps your mouth waters. Maybe the glands in the back of your throat get activated. Do you pucker? Are your teeth sensitive? Notice what happens as you bite into the lemon.

How was your experience? Could you "feel" the kitchen floor beneath your feet? Could you "see" your kitchen...your cabinets...the lemon? Could you smell or taste the lemon? What happened when you imagined biting into the lemon?

By using your imagination in the above exercise, you had a physical reaction or experience. That is how powerful your imagination is.

Ask athletes or performers and they will tell you that visualizing is an important part of their success. When you visualize you use your imagination to see the goal happening. You experience the details of the event before it actually takes place. Visualizing paints a vivid picture in your mind, allowing your goal to come alive.

To stimulate your imagination write down your goals and dreams. Before you sit down to write, clear your mind. Try not to edit or limit your thinking in any way. No one ever needs to read what you write so let your thoughts and dreams flow no matter how 'silly' or 'impossible' they may seem. Set your imagination free. You might surprise yourself with ideas you didn't even know you had.

Here are some additional tools for exercising your imagination:

- Spend time in nature. Marvel at the detail of a tiny flower or the majestic quality of an old oak tree.
- Spend time with a child. Play make-believe with him or her.
- Watch movies or read books that spark the imagination.
- Keep a dream journal. Record your dreams each morning as soon as you wake in order to remember as much detail as possible.
- Paint, draw, or sculpt. Be free with your creativity.
- Write a short story or describe in detail a dream come true. Be as descriptive as possible.

If limiting thoughts arise while imagining what you desire, try replacing them with more encouraging thoughts:

Limiting thought: 'I'm too busy to focus on my dreams.'

Encouraging thought: 'I allow my dreams to become part of my life.'

Limiting thought: 'It's just not realistic.'
Encouraging thought: 'Anything is possible!'

Limiting thought: 'I've always wanted to…but now it's too late.'
Encouraging thought: 'I'll never know unless I try. My life is my creation.'

"The world is but a canvas to our imaginations."
—Henry David Thoreau

Clarity

> "Clarity precedes success."
> —Robin Sharma

The process of achieving your dreams is simpler when you are clear about what you want and why you want it. Action is more easily taken when you know exactly what you are moving towards.

Often, people speak in generalized terms when describing what they desire. One might say, "I want to be rich," "I want to be married" or "I wish I had more time to myself." Become clear by asking specific questions: What will this bring me? How will I feel? When do I see it happening? Why do I want this in my life?

For example, instead of simply wishing "I want to be rich," be specific with the amount, the time frame and the reason behind the desire. Explore *why* you want to be rich. What do you think being rich will bring you? How will you feel? What do you hope to gain from the experience of being rich?

Instead of saying "I want to be married," ask yourself what qualities are important to you in another person. What kind of interests and values will he or she have? How do you see your lives unfolding and developing, both short and long-term? How will being married enrich your life and what do you envision yourself bringing to the relationship?

Instead of simply saying "I wish I had more time to myself," specify all the things you want to do with the extra time. Will you relax? Read? Play with your children? Paint? Cook? Meditate? Exercise? Why is it important to you to pursue these activities? The clarity you gain by asking these types of questions makes you more likely to follow through with your goals. When you know *why* you want something, you are more motivated to pursue it.

The GROUP

The following story shows how Glenn gained clarity regarding his job situation. He looked at not only *what* he wanted, but also *why* he wanted it.

> *Glenn graduated from university with a fine arts degree and was excited when he began working in an art gallery. He was surrounded by incredible artwork and was meeting talented artists. Yet it was not long before Glenn grew restless in his new job. The gallery was quiet and lonely, and he was not making as much money as he had hoped. He became clearer regarding what he wanted: "I want more excitement and more interaction with people so I don't feel as lonely. I want to be paid more so that I can save some money, not just pay my bills."*
>
> *He took a class in bartending and began working at a busy nightclub. The atmosphere was exciting, he was meeting lots of people, and he was making more money. However, after a few months, the job started to take a toll on Glenn. The hours were long and late, he was*

tired during the day, and he was not seeing his friends and family enough. He became clearer: "I love art and want to use my artistic ability because this is what fulfills me. I don't mind long hours, but I want to work during the day so I'm not so tired. I want a career that pays well and combines art and business."

With this increased clarity, Glenn took classes in commercial art and began a career in advertising. He now works with creative people, finds his career exciting and fulfilling, makes more money, and enjoys evenings and weekends with friends and family.

Glenn's story shows the importance of clarity and the value of continuing to move forward. His story also illustrates that there are no wrong decisions or directions — only opportunities to gain more clarity. During the process of gaining clarity, it is okay to make decisions and then change direction. The key is to *keep moving forward.* With each move Glenn made, he became clearer, eventually finding the ideal work situation.

The following two examples show how to be clearer about what you want and the importance of discovering why you want it.

Abstract:
"I want more free time."

Clearer:
"Twice a week, I want to spend two hours either gardening, painting, or spending time with friends."

Why?
"When I take time for myself in this way, I feel happier and healthier. These activities counter my stress and leave me feeling rejuvenated. When I feel better I'm more productive at work and more patient with my family."

Abstract:
"I want to make a difference in the world."

Clearer:
"I want to volunteer three hours a week at an animal shelter."

Why?
"I love animals. I want to give these animals love and attention. When I'm around animals I am pulled

out of my day-to-day problems and pulled into the moment. They make me smile. I feel like I've contributed to their well-being when I help them."

Clarifying your goals paints a detailed picture in your mind. These details help your visions become reality.

> "I don't care how much power, brilliance or energy you have, if you don't harness it and focus it on a specific target and hold it there, you're never going to accomplish as much as your ability warrants."
> —Zig Ziglar

Belief

"You can have anything you want if you will give up the belief that you can't have it."
—Dr. Robert Anthony

In order to achieve your dreams, you must believe that you can achieve them. Once you have belief in the possibility of achieving your dreams, little can stop you from reaching them. It may be helpful to start small. The only difference between manifesting "small" goals and "large" goals is the difference you create in your mind. If you begin by manifesting something small your confidence and belief will strengthen.

Uncertainty about your ability to manifest may sound like this:

Maybe…

I wish I could…

I hope…

If I'm lucky…

But how?

Believing you can accomplish what you want sounds like this:

I know…

I can…

I will…

I believe…

Many successful people do not realize they are "manifesting." Success seems to come naturally because they believe it is possible to accomplish what they set out to do. This belief enables them to consistently take action steps towards their goals.

Foster the belief that you have the power to create — because you do. We all do.

The following story illustrates how Mirja, one of the authors, fulfilled her dream of traveling to Africa:

Dreaming of Africa

For 12 years I had dreamed of traveling to Africa. I wanted to make a difference in the world. In 2004, I searched the Web and one research project in particular caught my attention, the Earthwatch Desert Elephants of Namibia expedition. I held elephants close to my heart. To contribute to their well-being and to our earth would be an enormous opportunity and a dream come true. As I read the briefing, excitement filled my entire body. I knew this project was the one.

The thought of the expedition and what it entailed scared me as much as it excited me. I would travel alone to Africa, which I had never before visited. I would live with only the basics, camping in the desert and cooking over a fire without any electricity. For me, this required courage and a quelling of 'what if' fears. I questioned whether I could really do this. Could I take action to make this dream a reality?

I kept the Earthwatch briefing next to my computer. Other papers eventually collected and were stacked on top of it. Daily life continued and weeks, months and years passed. I wanted to join the expedition in Namibia, but I just didn't know how...until we created our group in August 2006.

During one of our first meetings when I was honored, I surprised myself with what I shared with my GROUP. The dream from deep within my heart revealed itself again. I explained how I wished to make a difference in the world. I wanted to travel to Africa to study elephants. I wanted to make the change in my life that would inspire me to take action.

What was it that was keeping me from following my dream of going to Africa? The GROUP helped me with fresh perspectives, supportive questioning and encouragement. I found that I wasn't the only one with doubts, fears and obstacles. New insights revealed that I needed to change my way of thinking.

One of the biggest obstacles was my own mindset and fear. I realized that I did not have a strong enough belief that I could set out on frontiers unknown to me. The belief of 'yes, I can' is what I wanted to have. I recognized that I had a choice to believe in myself. This realization was the beginning of new courage and a new belief — the belief in my ability to go to Africa.

I began to take action. In September 2006, I paid the deposit to Earthwatch. I wasn't completely confident that I was going to go, but I took a step and it felt incredible! I continued taking action. I wrote down my thoughts on why I felt inspired to join the expedition and how I could manifest the trip. I thought about the adventure and the contribution

I would make. Encouragement surrounded me as family, friends and clients shared their travel experiences, tips and books. I envisioned myself sitting quietly looking out on the vast Namib Desert at sunrise. Step by step, thought by thought, meeting by meeting, my courage grew and I knew that I was definitely going.

My previous belief had kept me from traveling to Africa. I changed this. I now believed I could. In June 2007, with my gear packed and courage within me, I departed for Namibia. I made my dream come true!

> "Keep your dreams alive. Understand to achieve anything requires faith and belief in yourself, vision, hard work, determination and dedication. Remember, all things are possible for those who believe."
>
> —Gail Devers

Flexibility

"Be clear about your goal but be flexible about the process of achieving it."

—Brian Tracy

There are many different ways to achieve your dreams. When you are focused on one particular way of achieving what you want, opportunities can be missed. Be flexible and willing to accept progress in whatever form it may come.

Many people become attached to how they *think* they are going to achieve their goals. Do not be too "locked in" to *how* your goal will come to you. Many different paths can lead you to the same result. Be flexible and open to the possibility of obtaining your goal in a completely unexpected way. Be open to synchronicities, chance encounters and coincidences. Trust any hunches or feelings. Keep your eyes and your mind open and be ready for any avenues that "appear" that will lead you closer to your goal. Also, be flexible and open to the idea that something even better than your original idea may be coming to you.

The following story illustrates how Rebecca, one of the authors, came to own a luxury car by remaining flexible.

Manifesting a Luxury Car

> *"I want a Lexus 430 LS." I said this out loud for the first time at our GROUP meeting. Doubt immediately flooded my mind. Manifesting a car? Not just any car, but an expensive, beautiful car — the kind of car I have never owned, or even thought I could own. Was that even possible? My GROUP assured me that it was. With their support and their belief, my belief in the possibility began to grow.*

In the days that followed our meeting, something interesting happened. One after another, I encountered different people who presently or previously owned this particular Lexus. Every person had also owned an Infiniti. While they liked the Lexus, they loved the Infiniti more. They said it was the best luxury car they had ever owned. The model that several people mentioned was the Q45t.

I was intrigued. I went online to look at the Infiniti Q45t. A silver car appeared on the screen. It was beautiful! The interior had wood grain, tan leather seats and was plush and inviting. "Wow," was all I could muster when I saw that it was a $49,000 car. In the days that followed — despite the price tag — my energy, thoughts and attention were focused on that silver Infiniti Q45t.

A few days later, my husband, Mike, and I were with my father. We passed an Infiniti in a parking lot. I told my father that I was going to own one of those cars. With surprise and raised eyebrows, he replied, "Oh, really?" I told him, yes, really, and that I planned to test drive one next week. Again, raised eyebrows. Then I said something I never would have said to my father in the past. "And money is no object because I'm going to manifest it." My father is a pragmatic and skeptical man. In the past I would have worried that he would have thought me silly or impractical, but something made me say this anyway!

Later that same evening, my father said, "Wait a minute. Rebecca, do you remember Lloyd? He is selling his Infiniti." My eyes grew wide. Mike and I stared at each other. I asked my father if he had Lloyd's number and he did. He called Lloyd immediately and asked him if the Infiniti was still available, and it was. Mike and I were in the background saying, "Ask him what kind it is! Ask him what kind it is!" My father asked, waited for the answer, looked up from the phone, and said, "It's a Q45t."

It was the same beautiful silver color with tan leather seats and wood grain — exactly like the one I had seen online and exactly like the image I had been holding in my mind. The Infiniti had only 40,000 miles on it, had been garage kept and was like new. Lloyd was wealthy and owned a few cars, and although he loved the Infiniti, he said he just wasn't using it enough. He was selling it for only $11,000, and I bought it! After selling my car, I ended up paying only $6,500 for my Infiniti.

I'm a believer! How could I not be? I manifested a luxury Infiniti Q45t in only two months. With the help of my GROUP and their belief that it could happen, I began to believe...and it happened. By being flexible and open, and by trusting and believing...it happened. By following the feeling to tell my father what I was going to do...it happened. That is manifesting, and that is what brought me to my new car.

Every time I get in the driver's seat, put the key in the ignition and drive my Infiniti down the road, I am reminded that anything is possible.

In order to be flexible, remind yourself to look at all options. Be open to any and all possibilities. Remember, there are always many ways to achieve your goals.

> "When one door closes another door opens; but we so often look so long and so regretfully upon the closed door, that we do not see the ones which open for us."
>
> —Alexander Graham Bell

Trust

> "To sit patiently with a yearning that has not yet been
> fulfilled, and to trust that fulfillment will come,
> is quite possibly one of the most powerful 'magic skills'
> that human beings are capable of. It has been noted
> by almost every ancient wisdom tradition."
> —Elizabeth Gilbert

Imagine how your life would change if you let go of doubt and began to trust. Trusting that everything is working towards your highest good, even if it does not seem that way at the time, is essential to the process of manifesting. Your trust in the manifesting process can grow quickly once you begin to see results. In the meantime, practice fostering trust. If you are having difficulty trusting that you will achieve what you want, simply affirm to yourself, "I trust." There is power behind these two simple words. Trust that you will achieve what you want, *or something better*, and you will.

The following story illustrates how Rebecca, one of the authors, replaced fear and worry with trust:

Anything is Possible

I had been happily practicing hypnotherapy in an ideal business location just a few minutes from my home. One day, due to administrative changes, I learned that this office space would no longer be available. Almost immediately, I could feel fear and worry begin to surface: Where would I go? Could I find another space that I could afford? Would I lose my clients during the transition?

Although I was worried, for the first time in my life I did not let the fear take over. I reminded myself of what I was learning in my GROUP meetings: Trust...even when it feels difficult to do so.

Together with my GROUP, I became clear on what I wanted to create:

- *A professional space to practice*
- *No one to report to*
- *A great location, preferably in the larger town south of where I lived*
- *A very quiet and peaceful space*
- *No monthly rent; only paying when I occupied the space*

It all seemed reasonable until the last condition — no monthly rent? Was I being too unrealistic? Do places like that exist? My GROUP didn't blink an eye.

With their belief that it could happen, my belief grew. When I began to worry that it wouldn't happen or feel anxious about losing business, I would remind myself of what I learned during our meetings: Just trust. I am supported. Everything is perfectly timed. Follow any feelings. Take action. Anything is possible.

One day, the name of an acquaintance popped into my mind. I had the thought, 'Ask her about office space for rent.' Initially I thought, 'Why her? That makes no sense.' But I trusted the feeling and emailed her. She replied, "Come see me on Monday."

She put me in contact with someone who had a space. It was exactly what I was looking for. It was professional and I didn't have to report to anyone. It was in the perfect location in the town just south of me. It was peaceful and quiet. AND...I only had to pay a fee when I used the space.

This happened in just three weeks. By replacing fear with trust, my mind remained clear and calm, transforming an otherwise stressful experience into a smooth and easy transition to a great new office.

By trusting and keeping a clear mind, Rebecca ended up with exactly what she wanted. Wouldn't it be great if life always worked this way? But what if it had not worked out in this ideal way? What if, despite trusting and taking action steps, she had not been able to find an affordable space in which to practice?

Continuing to trust, even when you are not receiving what you want, takes you to a different *and deeper* level of trust. This deeper level of trust comes about by believing that one or both of the following statements are true:

Sometimes what you think you want is not what you are meant to have.

You are not receiving what you want because there is something better on the way.

You may have felt upset about an event not working out the way you wanted. Maybe you wanted something and didn't get it or something did not go your way. Then, a few weeks, months, or years later, you understood why you did not get what you had so badly wanted. Often the reasons why are not apparent until much later. You may even be *thankful* that you did not get what you wanted.

Steve's situation illustrates this clearly:

Steve had been in an "on and off" relationship with Rachel for three years. They broke up and got back together more times than Steve could remember. Because Steve was in his late 30's and wanted a family, he had some fears about getting older and not being able to find the "right" person. He wanted the relationship to work with Rachel but whenever they were together conflicts would arise.

The final breakup was hard for Steve. He knew they would not get back together again. The next few months were difficult for him. He second-guessed his decision and was tempted to call Rachel to see if they could make the relationship succeed. He worked on trusting that he was doing the right thing by not calling her, even though it wasn't easy for him.

Four months later, Steve met Celina. They had an instant connection. They both felt they were meant to be together. Their relationship was smooth and enjoyable. Two years later, they were married and now have a son.

Looking back, Steve realizes that if he had persisted with want he thought he wanted — continuing a relationship with Rachel — he never would have met Celina and would not be as happy as he is today. He trusted, even though things were not happening the way he wanted them to happen.

Trusting at this deeper level can take you beyond labeling an event as "good" or "bad" when it does not work out the way you want it to. Steve's loss became his gain. Trusting that everything is how it is supposed to be is a powerful practice. This is a reminder to *continue trusting* even when it is most difficult to do so. Trust that the process of life is working for your "highest good" even when it might not seem this way through your perspective. We may never know the bigger picture. We may never understand why things happen the way they do. Practice trusting even in the midst of disappointment. Learn to trust that there are positives hidden in seemingly "negative" situations. Practicing trust in this way opens the door to life's richest lessons and greatest opportunities. There is a gift or lesson in everything if we are open to seeing it.

> "Practice trust in that everything
> is just the way it is supposed to be."
> —Jose & Lena Stevens

Action

"He who has begun is half done."

—Horace

You have imagined. You have dreamed. You have become clear on what you want and believe you can have it. Now it is time to take action steps. To have achieved your dreams is to have taken action.

As you begin taking steps towards your goal, do not be hard on yourself. Do not worry about how big or small the step is. Do not worry about making mistakes when taking action. Movement in any direction creates momentum. Congratulate yourself on taking a step. It is better to take action — any action — than to sit on the fence, afraid that you might make the wrong move.

> *"As you begin to take action toward the fulfillment of your goals and dreams, you must realize that not every action will be perfect. Not every action will produce the desired result. Not every action will work. Making mistakes, getting it almost right, and experimenting to see what happens are all part of the process of eventually getting it right."*
>
> – Jack Canfield

Keep moving forward. When you have an idea that will bring you a step closer to your goal, act on it. You may have an idea that seems to come out of nowhere. When this happens, follow your idea. Take that step!

If you find that you are not inspired with an idea, take an action step anyway. What is *one thing* you can do right now that will bring you closer to your goal? Just one thing…do it now…take the first step. This action creates momentum towards achieving your dream. Now, imagine the momentum that is created when you have a group of people behind you, supporting you, believing in you, and encouraging you.

Using imagination and visualization as first steps and then following through with action, Tiffany, one of the authors, came to own her dream home:

Our Dream Home

My fiancé, Ian, and I traveled to Japan. I was moved by the splendor of the Japanese landscape, the harmoniously designed koi ponds and the tranquil meditation gardens. During the trip, I decided I wanted to capture what I saw in Japan and create a Zen-like atmosphere in my garden in Florida.

We had been thinking about buying a new home for months and upon our return we began the search. We spent several hours each day searching the Internet and driving through neighborhoods looking for the house. With each house we looked at I imagined how a Japanese garden would look in it. I talked about my garden idea with friends. I dreamt about it. I looked at pictures of Japanese landscaping.

Manifesting 63

After several months of searching, our realtor wanted to show us a house slightly out of our price range. For some reason, we agreed to see it. As soon as we walked in the front door I knew it had the potential to be our new home. As we walked through the dining room and peered onto the porch through the beautiful french doors, a lush garden of various flowering trees and shrubs appeared before us. My heart ignited as I walked onto the stepping stones. In front of my eyes was a pergola covered with Japanese honeysuckle that housed a beautiful bubbling waterfall and a large pond stocked with colorful koi fish. I couldn't believe it; I had never seen a garden like this in Florida. This was my Japanese garden! I had been dreaming of a garden like this for months. However, I thought I would have to build it myself. I never imagined that what I had pictured in my mind already existed.

Although the house was out of our price range, we were determined to make this dream a reality. In the weeks that followed we wondered how we were going to make this happen. Synchronistically, Ian's parents, who live in England, called unexpectedly during this time. They were looking forward to spending more time in Florida when they retire. Therefore, they wanted to help us invest in a bigger house should we ever decide to move.

The timing of their offer was perfect. All we had to do next was convince the owners to accept the offer we could now afford. We sat down and wrote a heartfelt, handwritten letter to the owners. A few days later they accepted our offer. Later we learned from the realtor that originally the owners were not going to budge on their price but upon reading our letter, something moved them. They wanted us to have the house.

I know that the desire and focus we had were what led us to this home. Taking action and believing in the process allowed all the other components to fall in place. Finding my garden taught me to let go of the limitations I had placed on myself. And to expect the unexpected.

"Success seems to be connected with action.
Successful people keep moving.
They make mistakes, but they don't quit."
—Conrad Hilton

3

Creating The Ideal GROUP Atmosphere

Creating the ideal GROUP atmosphere is vital to the success of your meetings. The members of your GROUP create this atmosphere. What can *you* do to ensure that your GROUP will be the best that it can be? Foster qualities in yourself that will help you be an asset to your GROUP. Cultivating the qualites listed below creates an environment where everyone, including yourself, can grow, share, achieve...and dream limitlessly.

Members of an effective GROUP can do the following, or are willing to learn how to:

1. Actively listen
2. Hold the space

3. Give and receive support and encouragement
4. Develop trust within The GROUP
5. Suspend judgment and practice acceptance of self and others
6. Be open
7. Celebrate the success of others
8. Avoid misinterpretation: take things the "right" way
9. Be patient
10. Be respectful
11. Bring out the best in others
12. Take responsibility
13. Be present

1. Actively listen

Active listening is one of the most important qualities to practice at your GROUP meetings. Excellent listeners create a powerful GROUP atmosphere. See Chapter 4, *Active Listening: The Key to Understanding Others*, to learn how to improve your listening skills.

2. Hold the space

When you "hold the space" for someone, you practice excellent listening skills, patience, understanding, and kindness. Holding the space is a way of listening that allows the speaker time and "space" to completely express his or her thoughts. It involves letting people find their own words in their own time. There may be pauses as the person searches for the right words. Allow the silence. Remain quiet and simply listen.

Holding the space allows the person speaking to express his or her thoughts and emotions without being interrupted. Interruptions include interjecting your own thoughts and opinions or physically hugging or touching the speaker. Physical touch, in an attempt to comfort someone, can be distracting and stop the flow of thoughts and emotions.

Holding the space is:

- Listening without interruption
- Allowing the speaker enough time to fully explore and express his or her thoughts
- Allowing pauses as the speaker searches for words

- Listening intently and being present for whomever is speaking
- Letting emotions arise and be processed without trying to stop them
- Asking questions at the appropriate time to gain understanding

Holding the space is **not:**

- Jumping in with solutions or advice
- Sharing your story
- Assuming that you understand or can offer guidance before the speaker is finished
- Telling someone what he or she should do
- Letting your mind wander while someone is speaking
- Becoming impatient if, in your opinion, the speaker is taking too long
- Physically comforting the person speaking when emotion arises

Below are two conversations. You will notice a difference between the two of them. Conversation #1 is an example of *not* holding the space, while conversation #2 demonstrates holding the space.

Conversation #1: *Not* Holding the Space

Tammy: "I'm struggling with a situation at work. One of my co-workers is making my days very difficult."

Erica: "Office settings are so tough sometimes."

Tammy: "My co-worker has a very negative attitude and complains most of the day. She's also not pulling her weight around the office."

Erica: "I hate that. I worked with someone like that."

Tammy: "I've been trying to stay positive but it's wearing me down. This woman saps my energy and I'm dreading being around her more and more."

Erica: "I know exactly what you're going through. I worked with this guy a few years ago who was just like that. Negative, lazy, not doing his fair share. He used to make me crazy! You know what I did? I went to my boss. I diplomatically explained the situation."

Tammy: "I feel like I need to do *something* because I'm not sure how much longer I can work like this. But I don't know if going to my boss is an option. You see, it's kind of a delicate situation. My boss –"

Erica: *(interrupting)* "If you don't do something about this, it's only going to get worse. People don't change unless you address the problem. It's not fair to you or to anyone else at the office. Go to your boss and explain what has been going on. Your boss will respect you for addressing the situation."

Conversation #2: Holding the Space

Tammy: "I'm struggling with a situation at work. One of my co-workers is making my days very difficult. She has a negative attitude and complains most of the day. She's also not pulling her weight around the office. I've been trying to keep positive but it's wearing me down. This woman saps my energy and I'm dreading being around her more and more. I'm not sure what to do."

Erica: "Are you around her often? Or are you around her just at certain times of the day or during certain tasks?"

Tammy: "I have to work directly with her quite often. I don't know how much longer I can work in this situation. It's really draining me. Something has to change."

Erica: "What are your options in this situation?"

Tammy: "Well, let's see... I don't know, actually. I feel trapped. I'm not sure what to do."

Erica: "Take your time. Even if it's not something you may follow through with, what are some of your options?"

Tammy: *(She is quiet for a few moments while she's thinking)* "Okay, I've got some options. I could quit. I could talk with the woman about the situation. I could talk to my boss, maybe. But there may even be some things I could do myself — like changing the way I think about it, or using it as an opportunity to practice patience."

Erica: "That's great, Tammy. Let's look at your options in more detail." *(By expanding on the above options, Tammy was able to decide which ones were not likely to have positive outcomes and which ones were.)*

In conversation #2, Erica gave Tammy "space" to find her words and express her thoughts. Erica asked questions at the appropriate times to help bring out more information and to help Tammy look inside herself for answers.

When someone is sharing, you may have a tendency to want to "fix" the problem. You may think, "How can I solve this problem for him?" or "What can I say to make her feel better?" Simply holding the space and *really* listening can often be more beneficial than giving advice.

Below is another example of the contrast between *not* holding the space and holding the space. During a GROUP meeting, Chloe shares a rediscovered passion to work with abused children.

Conversation #1: *Not* Holding the Space

Chloe: "I realize now that I want to help abused children. Volunteering at an abused children's shelter is something I used to tell myself I would do someday. I've always wanted to… *(tears well up in her eyes)* … It's important for me to…"

Chloe begins to cry and in an effort to comfort her, Dave places his hand lightly on top of her hand.

Dave: "It's okay Chloe, it's alright."

With this comfort from Dave, Chloe takes a deep breath and stops crying.

Dave: "It's never too late, Chloe. You should follow your dreams. I know of an abused women and children's shelter on 85th Street. You should go down there tomorrow and see how you can become a volunteer."

With Dave's advice, Chloe nods her head and agrees.

Dave, wanting to help Chloe, comforted her and offered a solution to her problem. This *seems* helpful because Chloe stopped crying and nodded in agreement with his suggestion. However, Dave did not "hold the space" for Chloe. He did not allow her to fully express her thoughts and emotions. He also did not allow her the opportunity to explore her options and come up with her own solutions.

Below is an example of Dave holding the space for Chloe. Doing this allowed Chloe to understand her emotions and move through them.

Conversation #2: Holding the Space:

Chloe: "I realize now that I want to help abused children. Volunteering at an abused children's shelter is something I used to tell myself I would do someday. I've always wanted to… *(tears well up in her eyes)*… It's important for me to…"

Chloe begins to cry. Her group remains silent and listens, allowing her to cry. They are holding the space.

After a few moments her crying subsides. With a deep breath, she sighs. She looks up at her group and smiles.

Dave: "Can you tell us about the emotion you were just feeling?"

Chloe: "When I was in college, I volunteered at a children's shelter. I grew very close to some of the children. It was an emotional time for me. Most of the children were so eager to be loved. Their struggles would break my heart but when I would bring a smile to one of their faces, I really felt like I was making a contribution. After college, I told myself that I would work with abused children again someday but I let my career take priority. I feel like I have somehow let the children and myself down."

Dave: "How would you feel if you were to volunteer at a children's shelter again?"

Chloe (*pausing, with tears in her eyes*)**:** "It would give me a deep sense of purpose again. I would feel like I was doing my part to make the world a better place. It would bring a smile to my heart. And more importantly, it would bring smiles to the children's hearts."

Dave: "What do you think those children, all grown up now, would say about you and what you did for them while you were in college?"

Chloe: "They would probably say, 'thank you for being there. It made a difference.'"

Chloe's face softens and she smiles.

Chloe: "I didn't let those children down, I helped them. I did the best I could at the time. I started my life after college. Now I am settled and I have even more time to devote to helping children again."

When Chloe's GROUP members held the space for her, her desires, fears, and solutions surfaced naturally. Her GROUP, by doing their part and holding the space, set the process of healing in motion. The GROUP enabled Chloe to answer her own questions and solve her own problems.

3. Give and receive support and encouragement

Encourage your fellow members. Be the support system that helps them rise to their highest potential. Remind them of their strengths and their accomplishments. Even the smallest step towards a goal is a success.

Work on fostering a positive and nurturing environment. When offering constructive feedback always be compassionate. Avoid criticizing. Focus on finding each other's strengths, acknowledging efforts and celebrating improvements. There are no failures, only opportunities to grow from every experience.

Your ability to *receive* support and encouragement is equally important. Some people have difficulty accepting a compliment. They may say, "No, that wasn't so great. I could have done better." If you don't feel good about yourself it can be hard to accept praise. Trust that your GROUP sees the good in you. Your GROUP believes in you; allow them to express how they feel. When you receive a compliment or encouragement, take a deep breath and accept their words as the truth.

By supporting and encouraging your GROUP members and allowing yourself to receive support and encouragement, you develop a stronger belief in yourself and your abilities. All things seem possible when we are encouraged.

4. Develop trust within The GROUP

It is important for The GROUP to cultivate an environment based on trust. There should be a commitment of confidentiality within The GROUP.

Whether it is verbalized or not, assume that everything shared at your meetings is private. A confidential environment is needed in order to speak freely. A level of comfort and freedom to be yourself is reached when you know that whatever you share will stay within The GROUP. Trust that your GROUP will keep everything you express private and show your fellow members the same courtesy. Over time trust will grow as you grow with one another.

5. Suspend judgment and practice acceptance of self and others

At times we may be hard on ourselves. We may have an underlying feeling that we are lacking in some way. This can cause us to be judgmental of ourselves and what we do. If we feel this way towards ourselves, it is not uncommon to also feel this way towards others. Be gentle with yourself. Allow yourself to be authentic during your meetings — faults, weaknesses, quirks and all. Have kindness and acceptance for yourself during your meetings and give that same gift to the members of your GROUP.

6. Be open

Practice openness with your GROUP. Allow yourself to say what is on your mind and in your heart. Be open to what others have to share. Do your best to consider all ideas. Be willing to explore all options.

Sometimes when you are facing a challenge or struggle in life it can be difficult to see your way out of it. There are times during your meetings when other members may offer ideas or suggestions. Some ideas will work and some will not, but do your best to keep an open mind and not rule anything out.

7. Celebrate the success of others

If you ever feel jealous or envious of what others have, you are not alone. In our competitive society, we are not typically taught to celebrate the success of others. Another's success can make us feel inadequate. We may put successful people down in an attempt to make ourselves feel better. If you feel jealous, use it as an opportunity to reflect on your own life. Is it possible that you are not taking enough action towards your own dreams and goals? What is it about the situation that makes you feel jealous and why?

It is easier to attract success when you are happy for the success of others. This ability to celebrate other's success opens you to more success of your own. *If another person can have it or do it, that means you can, too!*

A powerful advantage of being part of The GROUP is that the ability to celebrate other's success happens *naturally* — you do not have to force yourself to feel this way. The longer you are a member of The GROUP, the stronger this ability becomes. Imagine listening to a fellow member share a dream. At the next meeting, she shares a step she took towards this dream. Two meetings later, she announces that she has reached her goal! You are just as excited as she is because you supported, encouraged and believed in her. You were part of the process. When you offer support towards your GROUP members' dreams or simply listen and allow them to make their own discoveries, their accomplishments feel like your accomplishments. Illusory walls break down and are replaced by a sense of unity. You feel the connection that you share with your fellow human beings. When one person wins, we all win.

8. Avoid misinterpretation: take things the "right" way

We filter what is said to us through our own experiences, insecurities and beliefs. Because of this filtering process, it can be easy to misinterpret someone's words or actions. When we misinterpret or take things the "wrong" way, misunderstandings can easily arise.

It is important to remember that your GROUP cares about you. Your GROUP is here to help you and grow with you. Know that your GROUP wants you to succeed. Take everything that is said in the best possible way. Do your best not to misinterpret anything your fellow members say. If you have any question about something that was said, address it immediately. Most of the time the misunderstanding originates in our minds.

9. Be patient

Be patient during your meetings. Allow your fellow members to find their own words. Give each member time and space to express him or herself. Great discoveries and insights can arise from silence. Do not interrupt, finish sentences or rush the person speaking.

10. Be respectful

We all come from different backgrounds, experiences and belief systems. Although you may not fully agree with a fellow member's ideas or beliefs, do your best to see the value in his or her views and opinions. Be respectful of others' feelings and ideas.

11. Bring out the best in others

Compliment, support and encourage each other. See your fellow members as deserving, valuable and important. By valuing them in this way, you allow them to be their best selves. Believe in their abilities. Affirm your fellow GROUP members inherent worth and goodness. When you help to bring out the best in others, you bring out the best in yourself.

12. Take responsibility

The GROUP meetings are designed to inspire solutions, ideas and action steps. Therefore, it is helpful to have members who are positive, have open minds and who realize they are responsible for what they create in their lives. Members should be willing to learn from their mistakes and experiences. These meetings are *not* about blaming, complaining or playing the victim. The GROUP is successful when all members accept responsibility for themselves.

13. Be present

We all have busy lives and it is common to be preoccupied with our thoughts. Before each meeting begins, imagine any mental chatter dissolving or melting away. This can be challenging but becomes easier with practice. Take a deep breath and clear your mind. Listen intently when others are speaking. Be fully present for your GROUP.

One more recommendation

The GROUP meetings are goal-directed gatherings, not social events. Do not involve food or alcohol during these meetings as they can be distractions. You can always meet at other times to have a drink or share dinner together.

Practice	Avoid
Active listening	Talking too much, not listening
Holding the space	Interrupting, giving advice
Giving and receiving support and encouragement	Criticizing, downplaying achievements
Trusting	Breaching The GROUP's confidentiality
Acceptance	Judgment
Openness	Closed mindedness
Celebrating everyone's success	Jealousy, negativity
Taking things the "right" way	Misinterpreting
Patience	Impatience, interrupting
Respect	Dismissing other's views
Bringing out the best in others	Being unsupportive, focusing on shortcomings
Taking responsibility	Complaining, blaming, being the victim
Being present	A wandering mind, not listening

Beyond The GROUP

Creating the ideal GROUP atmosphere has advantages that reach far beyond helping others accomplish their goals. You begin to think more positively and listen more intently. You gain confidence. You believe in others and that belief is reflected back to you. You experience the benefit of being truly listened to, of being heard. You witness and experience dreams being accomplished. You create a bond with your GROUP members and a deep connection grows.

The empowerment you experience during your meetings flows into other aspects of your life. The positive changes that occur within you affect those around you — your family, your co-workers, and even strangers. Every area of your life will improve as a result of being part of The GROUP.

4

Active Listening: The Key to Understanding Others

> "I know that you believe you understand what you think I said, but I'm not sure you realize that what you heard is not what I meant."
>
> —ROBERT MCCLOSKEY

Listening, really listening *effectively*, is one of the greatest gifts you can give another person. One of the keys to a successful GROUP is "active listening." Active listening involves putting aside your own agenda and really hearing what another person is saying. Your goal is to understand the ideas and feelings of the person speaking. Improving your listening skills will not only benefit your GROUP, it will benefit all of your relationships, both professional and personal.

Think of active listening as "listening with your whole being." Be fully present for the person who is speaking. Focus all of your attention and energy on what the other person is saying. Do your best to keep your mind clear and quiet any "mental chatter" — any thoughts unrelated to what is being said.

Active listening involves:

- Allowing the person to speak without interruption and giving him or her the space to find the right words
- When appropriate, asking questions to gain clarity, more details, or a deeper understanding
- When necessary, restating in your own words what the other person is saying to make sure you understand

Some barriers that can interfere with your ability to listen are:

- Rehearsing
- Judging or Disagreeing
- Identifying (Telling Your Story)
- Advising
- Placating
- Dreaming

Rehearsing

Rehearsing is thinking about what you are going to say while the other person is still talking. You formulate a response in your mind and wait for the other person to stop talking so you can speak. When you rehearse you do not truly hear what the other person is saying.

Judging or Disagreeing

Judging is getting caught up in whether you agree or disagree with the other person's point of view. You do not necessarily have to *agree* with what the person is saying, but do your best to *understand* what he or she is saying.

Identifying (Telling Your Story)

Identifying involves telling your story to the person who is speaking. When someone is sharing something with you it may trigger an experience you had and you decide that now would be a great time to share your story. "Oh yeah, that happened to me, too! I know *exactly* what you mean," and you proceed to tell your story.

Identifying can also involve "one-upping." The person speaking tells you about an experience and then you say, "Oh, that's nothing. When I was there it was so much worse…" or different, or whatever makes your story better in some way.

Advising

Advising is being the problem solver. You may feel a need to have the right answers or want to impress the other person with your knowledge. You may feel the need to "fix" the problem. You may want to tell the person what he or she should do, what you would do in that situation, or what you have done in the past.

Placating

Placating is agreeing with everything that is being said, so that it seems like you are listening, but you are really only half listening. Sometimes "placaters" use words like, "right, right...yeah...um hmm...oh, really..."

Dreaming

Dreaming occurs when your mind wanders and you are off "dreaming" about something happening in your own life. For example, you are thinking about a conversation you had earlier, errands you have to run, or a deadline at work.

Anyone can become a better a listener with practice. Here are some helpful hints:

Focus solely on what the other person is saying
Most barriers to effective listening stem from a "busy mind." If your own thoughts jump in, notice them and let them go. Continue to bring your focus and attention back to what the person is saying. You may need to redirect your focus often in the beginning but it will become easier with practice.

Keep an open mind
Wait until the other person is finished speaking before you decide whether you agree or disagree. Suspend judgment. Try not to make assumptions about what the person is thinking or feeling.

Refrain from telling your story
It is important to listen attentively and refrain from interjecting comments or telling stories when someone else is speaking as this can disrupt the person's train of thought.

Ask, don't tell
Fight the urge to fix the problem or to give advice. Instead of telling the person what to do, you can ask questions to help the person find his or her answers. Unless the person specifically asks for advice, it is usually best not to give it — just be present and listen.

Think about how good it feels when someone is present for you and truly listens. You feel validated and supported. Paul Tillich, the German-American theologian and philosopher, said, *"The first duty of love is to listen."* You will find his words to be true as you hone your listening skills.[1]

5

The Structure of The GROUP Meeting

At the core of your GROUP meeting is a unique structure that creates a shift in thinking and supports the process of manifesting. This structure, consisting of five segments, was designed to promote gratitude, encouragement and success. Like building blocks, each segment builds upon the previous segment to inspire you to dream, motivate you to take action, and help you achieve your desired objective. The significance of each segment is explained in detail in this chapter.

The five segments of your meeting and their allotted times are as follows:

1. **Opening**
   15 minutes
2. **Gratitude**
   15 minutes
3. **Successes**
   15 minutes
4. **Honoring & Action Steps**
   60 minutes
5. **Closing**
   15 minutes

The suggested time for a meeting is two hours. An option for a large group (five or six people) is to hold a 2½ hour meeting. Instead of the above format for a 2 hour meeting with one person honored for 60 minutes, two people are honored for 45 minutes each.

OPENING

Led by the Guide
Length: 15 Minutes

1. The Guide welcomes The GROUP.
2. The Guide asks the Timer to explain the method of keeping time.
3. The Guide reads the Purpose.
4. The Guide reads the Offering and gives each member a copy.

The room becomes quiet. A feeling of excitement and anticipation emerges as everyone gathers. The meeting is about to begin.

The Guide begins the meeting by welcoming everyone and then asks the Timer to explain how the time will be kept.

The Guide reads the Purpose out loud during the Opening of every meeting. Hearts and minds are synchronized as everyone is reminded why they are there. The Purpose is written by your group members at the first meeting. For a full description of the Purpose, how to create your own, and examples of Purposes, see Chapter 7, *How to Form The GROUP.*

98 The GROUP

Next, the Guide reads the Offering and provides a copy to each member. The Offering can be a short inspirational story, a single quote or a collection of quotes, a favorite passage from a book, a parable, a teaching, or lyrics from a song. Any words of encouragement or inspiration work well. Inspirational stories lift our spirits and remind us that anything is possible. Amy shared the following Offering at our first meeting:

> *Some time ago, at the Seattle Olympics, nine athletes, all mentally or physically challenged, were standing on the start line for the 100 meter race. The gun fired and the race began. Not everyone was running, but everyone wanted to participate and win.*
>
> *As they ran, one boy tripped and fell, did a few somersaults and started crying. The other eight heard him crying. They slowed down and looked behind them. They stopped and came back. All of them...*
>
> *A girl with Down's Syndrome sat down next to him, hugged him and asked, "Feeling better*

now?" Then, all nine walked shoulder to shoulder to the finish line.

The whole crowd stood up and applauded. And the applause lasted a very long time.

People who witnessed this still talk about it. Why?

Because deep down inside us, we all know that the most important thing in life is much more than winning for ourselves.

The most important thing in this life is to help others to win. Even if that means slowing down and changing our own race.[2]

GRATITUDE

Led by the Guide
Sharing by All Members
Length: 15 Minutes

1. The Guide chooses a person to begin.
2. Each person (including the Guide) shares 1–3 Gratitudes, keeping in mind that the other members need time to share as well.

Gratitude is a magnet. Sharing what we are grateful for empowers us. When we experience gratitude and give thanks for what we have, we invite more of the same into our lives.

If there are times when finding something to be grateful for seems difficult, you can begin by being grateful for small things, such as your cat, a smile from a stranger, or a flower. Feeling gratitude for the simplest of things helps you notice more things for which to be grateful. This practice quickly builds upon itself.

The Guide chooses who will begin this segment by calling on one of the members to start. By rotating

The Structure of The GROUP Meeting

in a circle, each person in The GROUP shares one to three things for which he or she is thankful. Notice the shift you feel when you focus your attention on things for which you are grateful. Notice the joy you feel for others as they do the same.

The following are examples of Gratitudes that we have shared during our meetings:

> "I am grateful for this group. These meetings keep me thinking and acting positively."
>
> "I am grateful for the abundance in my life and for good health."
>
> "I am grateful for yoga."
>
> "I am grateful for life's little surprises. Today, I found $1.75 worth of quarters at the car wash!"
>
> "I am grateful to be living in a peaceful society with endless choices and possibilities. I am grateful for my life."

Mirja, one of the authors, shares her realization of how abundance reveals itself in so many ways:

A Simple Gift

One afternoon, I stood in front of the postage stamp machine at the post office to avoid the long line. I didn't have much time and just wanted to purchase a single stamp for a bill I needed to mail that day. I took the only money I had in my pocket, a $5.00 bill, and inserted it into the slot. It immediately reappeared out of the slot. I reinserted it, and it reappeared. I tried again and there it was again.

I looked at the line, then looked at my watch and thought 'all I need is one stamp.' Right at that moment, a man who had been watching this while waiting for his wife, walked over. He placed a $10.00 bill in the machine, purchased a book of stamps and gave me the stamp I needed! I offered to get change out of my car to pay him back but he said it wasn't necessary. I thanked him and with gratitude I thought, 'now, that's abundance — a gift of money and time!'

SUCCESSES

Led by the Guide
Sharing by All Members
Length: 15 Minutes

1. The Guide chooses a person to begin.
2. Each person (including the Guide) shares 1–3 Successes, keeping in mind that the other members need time to share as well.

Celebrate your success! A success can be anything. You took a step toward a goal. Something motivated or inspired you. You finished an important project. You took much needed time to rest. You had an experience that brought about a new way of feeling, thinking or doing something.

When we think of what constitutes a success, we may think of things such as "I received a promotion" or "I bought my first house." Success is often thought of as an end result — as finally accomplishing a hard-earned goal. However, every step taken towards a goal is also a success. Small accomplishments create the foundation for large accomplishments. Acknowledge and celebrate your progress in whatever form it takes.

By acknowledging and witnessing success, a shift in one's mindset occurs. You learn to celebrate the success of others as well as cultivate more success in your own life. Your idea of what constitutes a success changes. As you become more aware of success — looking for it, talking about it and celebrating it — you will discover that success attracts more success.

The Guide chooses who will begin. By rotating in a circle, each person in The GROUP shares one to three successes. The person who was the Honored One during the previous meeting may wish to share a success that resulted from being honored.

Following are examples of Successes we have shared at our meetings:

"I exercised three times last week."

"I forgave myself for a mistake I made."

"I finally realized that stress is within my control. Stress is not something that 'happens' to me. I control whether or not I experience stress."

"I started drawing and painting again for the first time in many years."

*"I took a step toward a better financial future
by setting up automatic deposits into my
savings account each month."*

*"I took time out to walk on the beach yesterday
even though I felt like I had too much to do.
It ended up being exactly what I needed."*

Tiffany, one of the authors, shared this success at one of our meetings:

Overnight Success

One afternoon, I wrote down a list of short-term goals. I have found making lists helpful in keeping me moving in the direction of my goals. After I finished typing my list, I realized I had forgotten one item. For some time, I had wanted a beautiful new mountain bike. I added this item to the bottom of my list, hit save and went about my day.

The next day while I was at work a very dear client of mine stopped by the office. His timing was synchronistic because had he arrived five minutes earlier or later, I would have been with another client and would have missed him. He made a purchase and then asked me, "Do you want a bike?" Intrigued, I replied, "What kind of bike?" He said, "It's a bike I bought for my daughter. She isn't going to use it and I don't want it just sitting around my garage." "Is it a mountain bike?" I asked. He shrugged and said "I don't think so. I hesitated because I didn't want to take something I wouldn't use. Then he said, "I have it in the trunk of my car. Just come out and get it. If you don't want it, perhaps you know someone who does." That sounded like a good idea so we walked out to his car. He untied the rope from his trunk latch and before my eyes was a brand new woman's Trek mountain bike! It was so new that the wheels looked like they had never touched pavement.

I jumped with excitement when I saw the bike. "This is a great bike! It's exactly the kind I wanted!" My client seemed pleased to get the bike off his hands. I thanked him heartily and we said goodbye. As I pushed my new bike toward the office, I exploded with laughter and felt a wave of gratitude as I remembered the last addition to my list less than 24 hours ago. Now that's what I call overnight success!

HONORING & ACTION STEPS
Sharing by the Honored One
Participation from All Members
Length: 60 Minutes

1. The Honored One shares a dream, a goal, a challenge, or a desired change.
2. The GROUP actively listens and asks questions when appropriate.
3. The Action Step Writer takes notes in the Honored One's notebook.

Encouragement. Motivation. Collaboration. A group of people dedicated to listening to you and helping you. Imagine what you can accomplish in your life with this kind of support.

The Honoring segment is devoted to one person, the Honored One. The Honored One shares a challenge, a goal, a dream, or a change he or she wishes to make. As the Honored One, if you are not sure exactly what you wish to focus on, The GROUP can help you gain clarity. For full details on the Honoring segment refer to Chapter 6, *The Roles of The GROUP Meeting*.

The GROUP actively listens and "holds the space" while the Honored One shares thoughts and feelings. Once the Honored One has finished, the other GROUP members may ask questions to gain further insight and understanding. This process helps the person uncover any obstacles and move towards the goal on a physical, emotional, mental and spiritual level.

The Action Step Writer takes notes in the Honored One's notebook during this segment.

CLOSING

Led by the Guide
Sharing by All Members
Length: 15 Minutes

1. The Guide introduces the Closing and chooses a person to begin.
2. The first person states a goal.
3. Everyone closes his or her eyes and directs the focus towards that person.
4. The Timer keeps track of the time and says "thank you" at the end of two minutes.
5. By rotating in a circle, everyone (including the Guide) has a turn.

A feeling of joy, gratitude and peace fills the room as the meeting draws to a close. During the Closing, attention is directed towards each member achieving his or her goals, desires and dreams.

The Guide introduces the segment and calls on a member to begin. The person shares a goal. The goal may be one that the other members are familiar with or it may be something different. The goal can be something tangible such as a vacation, a car, or a specific type of job. It can also be something intangible such as a healing, forgiveness, a better understanding of an issue, loving oneself more...*anything*.

Immediately after the first member shares a goal, everyone closes their eyes and takes two minutes of silence to direct their focus, attention and energy towards that person. Each member can approach this process differently. Some people may visualize the person accomplishing the goal. Others may direct a feeling such as strength, support or encouragement toward the person. The person receiving the focus can visualize the goal being achieved or can simply sit quietly with eyes closed, open to receiving. There are no rules during this process. The GROUP can visualize and send thoughts or energy in whatever way feels most natural and powerful.

When multiple minds focus on the same intention there is a heightened energy that is created. Although this shift in energy can be subtle, you will quite often feel it during this segment. Power is derived from the synergy of The GROUP.

Below is an example from one of our meetings. Amy wanted to become pregnant. During the two

The Structure of The GROUP Meeting   111

minutes, this is what each member felt or held in her thoughts:

Tiffany imagined Amy announcing, "I'm pregnant!" Tiffany felt the joy and excitement within herself from this good news. She imagined everyone hugging and congratulating Amy.

Rebecca imagined Amy's stomach swollen with pregnancy. She saw Amy smiling, happy, touching her stomach, talking about the fast approaching due date.

Mirja directed loving energy towards Amy. She imagined a bright light filling Amy's stomach. She saw life there. She repeated in her mind, "Amy is pregnant, Amy is pregnant."

Amy quieted her mind and imagined receiving the thoughts and energy sent to her by her GROUP.

The Timer keeps track of the two minutes while participating in the process. When the two minutes for each person is up, the Timer says "thank you" and The GROUP moves on to the next person. By rotating in a circle, the process is repeated until everyone has had a turn. When the Timer shares a goal, another person keeps track of the two minutes. As the Closing ends, a feeling of connection is experienced. Peacefulness envelops everyone.

The meeting inspires you to begin the next day energized, renewed and ready to take action. It is as though a bridge has been created — a bridge from your meeting back into your life. This bridge provides the strength, the support, and the motivation to accomplish your dreams.

Shortly after she received the focus of our GROUP, Amy, one of the authors, shared a wonderful success:

I'm Pregnant!

When we formed The GROUP in August 2006, I had been trying to become pregnant for a year. I had grown increasingly worried and anxious that I would not be able to have a child. At 38 years old, I also became angry with myself. I scolded myself, saying "You fool. You waited too long. What were you thinking?" I went from being worried to distraught. The more it looked like I wouldn't be able to get pregnant, the more I obsessed and worried about it.

I shared all of this with my GROUP — my fear of not being able to have a baby and the stress I was experiencing because of it. Acceptance, trust and learning how to reduce stress were some of the insights that surfaced during that meeting. I took all I had learned home with me and put it into action. By accepting my situation and trusting that everything was the way it should be, I was able to relax and have a more positive outlook.

At our third meeting, as we were sharing our successes, I announced, "I'm pregnant!"

My GROUP helped me become aware of and clear away negative, self-defeating thoughts. I believe that this helped me relax and trust, which in turn helped me become pregnant. I now have a beautiful baby girl who has enriched my life in ways that I could never have imagined.

OUTLINE OF THE GROUP MEETING

Opening: 15 Minutes
Led by the Guide
1. The Guide welcomes The GROUP.
2. The Guide asks the Timer to explain the method of keeping time.
3. The Guide reads the Purpose.
4. The Guide reads the Offering and gives each member a copy.

Gratitude: 15 Minutes
Led by the Guide, sharing by All Members
1. The Guide chooses a person to begin.
2. Each person (including the Guide) shares 1–3 Gratitudes, keeping in mind that the other members need time to share as well.

Successes: 15 Minutes
Led by the Guide, sharing by All Members
1. The Guide chooses a person to begin.
2. Each person (including the Guide) shares 1–3 Successes, keeping in mind that the other members need time to share as well.

The Structure of The GROUP Meeting

Honoring & Action Steps: 60 Minutes
Sharing by the Honored One, participation from All Members
1. The Honored One shares a dream, a goal, a challenge, or a desired change.
2. The GROUP actively listens and asks questions when appropriate.
3. The Action Step Writer takes notes in the Honored One's notebook.

Closing: 15 Minutes
Led by the Guide, sharing by All Members
1. The Guide introduces the Closing and chooses a person to begin.
2. The first person states a goal.
3. Everyone closes his or her eyes and directs the focus towards that person.
4. The Timer keeps track of the time and says "thank you" at the end of two minutes.
5. By rotating in a circle, everyone (including the Guide) has a turn.

6
The Roles of The GROUP Meeting

The roles performed at your meetings can be infused with your own creativity. Having roles transforms an otherwise social gathering into a structured and purposeful meeting.

The roles to be fulfilled are:

GUIDE

TIMER

HONORED ONE

THE GROUP

ACTION STEP WRITER

GUIDE

What to Bring

- Your copy of the Purpose
- An Offering you have brought for the meeting
- Copies of the Offering to be handed out to each member
- A notebook and pen or pencil

What to Do

1. Open the meeting by welcoming everyone.
2. Invite the Timer to explain how the time will be kept throughout the meeting.
3. Read the Purpose.
4. Read the Offering and provide copies to each member.
5. Direct the flow of the meeting by introducing each segment. The Guide calls on a member to begin each segment.
6. Determine roles for the next meeting.

The Guide oversees the meeting by welcoming everyone, introducing each segment, and keeping

The Roles of The GROUP Meeting 119

the meeting on schedule. At the beginning of the meeting, the Guide invites the Timer to explain how the time will be kept. Once the method of keeping time has been explained, the Guide reads the Purpose out loud, and then reads the Offering. The Offering is brought by the Guide and can be a single quote, a collection of quotes, a short story, lyrics from a song or anything inspirational or motivational. The Guide provides copies of the Offering to each member. See *Our Offerings from The GROUP Meetings* for examples of Offerings we have brought to our meetings.

The Guide directs the flow of the meeting by introducing each segment. During the Gratitude, Success and Closing segments, the Guide calls on a member to begin. During the Honoring segment, the Guide invites the Honored One to begin.

At the end of each meeting, the Guide and The GROUP determine who will fulfill each role for the next meeting. The roles rotate amongst members from meeting to meeting. Depending on the size of The GROUP, some members may not have a role during every meeting, but they are still active participants. If The GROUP has less than four people, it will be necessary for a member to have more than one role.

TIMER

What to Bring

- A watch or clock with a second-hand timer
- 'Props' to keep track of the time
- A notebook and pen or pencil

What to Do

1. Explain how you will keep time at the meeting. The Guide will call upon you to explain at the beginning of the meeting.
2. At the beginning of each segment, write down the time the segment begins, the halfway point, the two minute point, and the time the segment will end. Writing this down is simply a note for yourself to help you keep track of the time.
3. With the 'props' you have brought, notify The GROUP of the halfway point, when there are two minutes left, and when the segment is over.

The five segments of the meeting each have a specific time allotment. The Timer's responsibility is to

The Roles of The GROUP Meeting 121

inform everyone of the time during each segment in order to keep the meeting on schedule. At the beginning of each meeting, when prompted by the Guide, the Timer explains how the time will be kept.

The Timer brings 'props' as a way of informing The GROUP of the time. Examples of props are candles, chimes, pictures, bells, signs, or anything you have created yourself. Choosing props and informing everyone of the time can be approached as simply or as creatively as you wish.

During each of the five segments the Timer informs The GROUP of the following:

1. The halfway point of the segment
2. When there are two minutes left in the segment
3. When the segment is over

This is an example of how the time was kept at one of our meetings:

The Timer brought three candles to use as props. The meeting started at 7:00 pm. The first segment, the Opening, is 15 minutes long, so it would end at

7:15 pm. The Timer lit the first candle half way through the segment at approximately 7:08 pm. This signaled to The GROUP that the segment was half way over. The second candle was lit at 7:13 pm, signaling that there were two minutes left in the segment. At 7:15 pm, the Timer lit the third candle, informing all members that the segment was over. It was time to wrap up and continue to the next segment of the meeting.

If The GROUP goes beyond the allotted time for a segment there can be flexibility, especially if someone is sharing something important. However, it is good practice to stay within the designated time frame. By covering the segments in a timely manner, the meetings begin and end on time. A specific time frame ensures that anyone can participate in The GROUP regardless of a busy schedule.

Have fun with this role and feel free to be creative with the time-keeping process.

HONORED ONE

What to Bring

- A notebook and pen or pencil
- A dream, goal, challenge, or desired change

What to Do

1. Be ready to share a dream, goal, challenge, or desired change with your GROUP.
2. Give your notebook to the Action Step Writer at the beginning of the Honoring segment.

The Honored One brings a dream, goal, challenge or desired change to the meeting. During the Honoring segment, the Honored One receives the focus of The GROUP. The topic of discussion can be anything, from the seemingly insignificant to something of vast importance — it can be as broad and varied as your imagination. Goals can be tangible and material or ethereal and philosophical.

Below are examples of topics brought to our meetings:
- Clarity regarding making a decision
- Relaxing more, reducing stress
- Becoming more artistic
- Healing a physical issue
- Making a career change
- Opening one's heart to more joy after the end of a relationship
- Greater responsiveness to one's intuition; trusting oneself
- Making more money
- Becoming pregnant
- Letting go of irrational fears, worries, and "what-ifs"
- Being more present
- Experiencing more inner peace

During this segment the Honored One has the opportunity to arrive at new possibilities and insights while sharing feelings and thoughts. The Honored One will benefit the most by being open, authentic and trusting.

THE GROUP

What to Bring

- A notebook and pen or pencil

What to Do

1. Actively listen, "hold the space," and ask the Honored One questions to gain clarity.
2. Ask the Honored One questions to activate the imagination and uncover obstacles.
3. Discuss action steps.

The role of The GROUP, including the Guide and the Timer, during the Honoring segment is to actively listen, "hold the space," and question the Honored One to gain clarity. This process involves three steps:

1. Clarifying the Honored One's Goal
2. Guiding the Honored One Inward
3. Discussing Action Steps

1. Clarifying the Honored One's Goal

In the beginning of the Honoring segment, the Honored One shares a dream, goal, challenge or a desired change. During this time, it is important for The GROUP to practice active listening. Do not interrupt the person being honored. Discoveries and insights can occur by allowing the Honored One to explore his or her thoughts and feelings. Long pauses may arise as the Honored One seeks to capture the essence of what he or she is saying. Allow the Honored One to find his or her own words. Allow as much time as needed. After the Honored One shares, it may be necessary for The GROUP to ask questions to gain a deeper understanding of the goal.

2. Guiding the Honored One Inward

At this point in the process, The GROUP becomes more actively involved. Questions can be asked to bring the desired goal to life. Good questions engage the mind and activate the imagination. Ask the Honored One what life will be like when the goal is a reality. This process helps bring the dream to life.

Examples of questions that activate the imagination are:

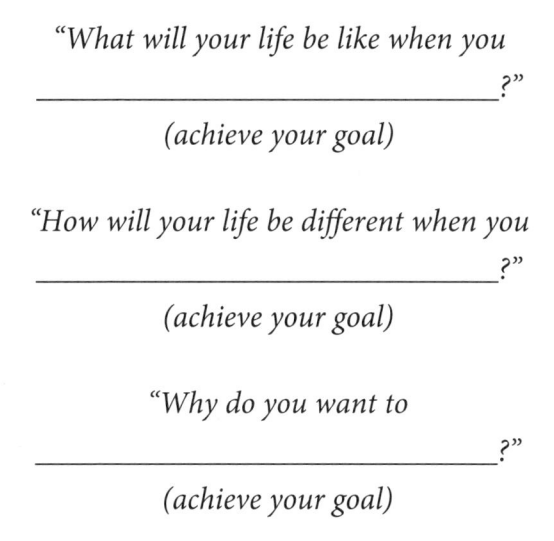

"*What will your life be like when you _____?*"
(achieve your goal)

"*How will your life be different when you _____?*"
(achieve your goal)

"*Why do you want to _____?*"
(achieve your goal)

It is also important to encourage the Honored One to get in touch with how it will feel when the goal has been accomplished. When you have an emotion attached to accomplishing a goal, you become more motivated, driven, and inspired to achieve that goal. Ask questions that help the Honored One get in touch with how the accomplishment will feel.

Examples of questions that can help are:

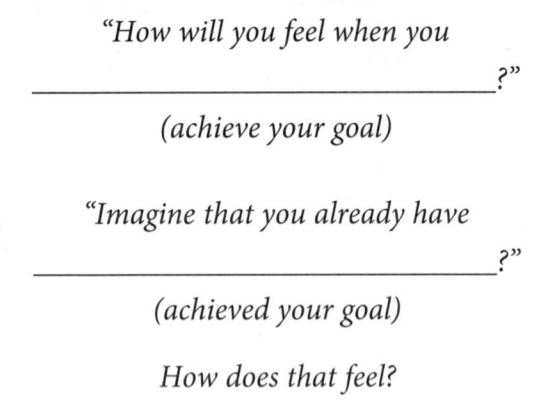

> "How will you feel when you _____?"
> *(achieve your goal)*

> "Imagine that you already have _____?"
> *(achieved your goal)*
>
> How does that feel?

The following question is important as it can access emotions and bring to light any fears or obstacles which may be preventing movement towards the goal.

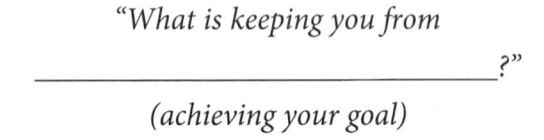

> "What is keeping you from _____?"
> *(achieving your goal)*

During this phase, fears, insecurities, doubts and perceived obstacles may come to light. It is important for The GROUP to let the Honored One process whatever emotion arises. If anger, frustration, tears, or any other kind of emotion surfaces, allow it to happen.

If emotions do arise, it is important not to comfort, hug or touch the person as this may interrupt the process. Let the Honored One have the experience and move through the emotions. It is natural to want to comfort someone, but by doing so, you may not allow the person to fully experience the emotion. By listening, holding the space and allowing the emotion to occur, you are giving the person a great gift.

Some examples of what you can say to help the Honored One move through any emotions that arise are:

> *"Tell me what you're feeling right now."*

> *"Tell me about that emotion."*

> *"I noticed that some emotion came up when you were talking about _____.
> Tell me more about that."*

Emotions can act as a guide, providing clues to what you are thinking. Once you understand what you are thinking, it becomes easier to uncover obstacles and move toward your goal.

3. Discussing Action Steps

Ask the Honored One what she can do to move towards her goal. We are more likely to follow through with something we say we will do if we are held accountable.

Examples of questions that encourage taking action are:

> *"What is one thing you can do before the end of the week that will bring you closer to your goal?"*

> *"What can you start doing differently tomorrow?"*

> *"What can you do by the next meeting that will help you move closer to accomplishing your goal?"*

The Honoring segments can feel like "brainstorming" sessions. The GROUP can offer their suggestions and ideas, although it is most beneficial to help the Honored One discover his or her own solutions. The ideas offered may consist of steps that can be taken, new perspectives or any insights. Not all ideas have to be accepted, but different options can be explored.

The support of The GROUP is essential. If the Honored One starts to doubt or focus on reasons why something cannot be done, The GROUP can step in and redirect the Honored One to a more positive outlook, reassuring him or her that movement towards the goal is possible. The emphasis is on solutions, possibilities and taking action.

Active listening is vital during this time. Keep the attention solely on the Honored One. There can be a temptation to share one's personal stories and express how they relate to the Honored One's situation, but doing this should be kept to a minimum. Do your best not to direct attention away from the Honored One.

If at times it seems as though you have not helped during the honoring process, be assured that you have. Simply by listening, allowing the Honored One to express him or herself, and holding the space, you have helped immensely.

ACTION STEP WRITER (ASW)
What to Bring
- A notebook and pen or pencil

What to Do
1. As the Honoring segment of the meeting is beginning, take the notebook of the Honored One.
2. Record notes in the Honored One's notebook. This includes, but is not limited to: thoughts and emotions relating to the goal, questions that arise, revelations or insights, obstacles or fears that surface, keywords and action steps that can be taken to reach the goal.
3. It is better to write down too much than too little.

The Action Step Writer (ASW) takes detailed notes for the Honored One throughout the Honoring segment. These notes assist the Honored One in taking action towards achieving the goal after the meeting. Although the ASW may participate with questions and suggestions, his or her main responsibility is to actively listen and record as much as possible in the Honored One's notebook. This allows the Honored One to be present, to process what surfaces, and to be open to what The GROUP contributes.

As the Action Step Writer, it is important to record as much as possible because you never know what may be significant to the Honored One. You may be writing almost constantly at times. It is better to write down more than you think may be needed than to leave out information. If you feel you are writing too much, then you are performing your role correctly. The best notes are thorough notes.

The ASW creates the road map the Honored One will use to begin the journey towards achieving his or her goal. The notes may include, but are not limited to, the following:

- The Honored One's goal and any details clarifying the goal
- Thoughts and feelings relating to the goal
- Questions posed by the Honored One or other members

- Revelations and insights by the Honored One and/or The GROUP
- Obstacles or fears that surface
- Keywords and meaningful phrases (e.g. "trust" or "acceptance")
- Suggestions and ideas
- Helpful resources (e.g. books, websites, organizations)
- Action steps that can be taken to achieve the goal
- A drawing or a symbol (e.g. The Honored One said that an aspect of her personality was "blooming." The ASW drew a flower with the Honored One's name next to it.)
- Inspiring words or encouraging phrases (e.g. "You can do it!" "We believe in you.")

CHECKLIST FOR EACH MEETING

GUIDE

What to Bring

- Your copy of the Purpose
- An Offering you have brought for the meeting
- Copies of the Offering to be handed out to each member
- A notebook and pen or pencil

What to Do

1. Open the meeting by welcoming everyone.
2. Invite the Timer to explain how the time will be kept throughout the meeting.
3. Read the Purpose.
4. Read the Offering and provide copies to each member.
5. Direct the flow of the meeting by introducing each segment. The Guide calls on a member to begin each segment.
6. Determine roles for the next meeting.

TIMER

What to Bring

- A watch or clock with a second-hand timer
- 'Props' to keep track of the time
- A notebook and pen or pencil

What to Do

1. Explain how you will keep time at the meeting. The Guide will call upon you to explain at the beginning of the meeting.
2. At the beginning of each segment, write down the time the segment begins, the halfway point, the two minute point, and the time the segment will end. Writing this down is simply a note for yourself to help you keep track of the time.
3. With the 'props' you have brought, notify The GROUP of the half-way point, when there are two minutes left, and when the segment is over.

HONORED ONE

What to Bring

- A notebook and pen or pencil
- A dream, goal, challenge, or desired change

What to Do

1. Be ready to share a dream, goal, challenge, or desired change with your GROUP.
2. Give your notebook to the Action Step Writer at the beginning of the Honoring segment.

THE GROUP

What to Bring

- A notebook and pen or pencil

What to Do

1. Actively listen, "hold the space," and ask the Honored One questions to gain clarity.
2. Ask the Honored One questions to activate the imagination and uncover obstacles.
3. Discuss action steps.

ACTION STEP WRITER (ASW)
What to Bring
- A notebook and pen or pencil

What to Do
1. As the Honoring segment of the meeting is beginning, take the notebook of the Honored One.
2. Record notes in the Honored One's notebook. This includes, but is not limited to: thoughts and emotions relating to the goal, questions that arise, revelations or insights, obstacles or fears that surface, keywords and action steps that can be taken to reach the goal.
3. It is better to write down too much than too little.

7
How to Form The GROUP

Starting The GROUP is one of the best decisions you will make. Get ready for wonderful things to happen in your life! By following the guidelines in this chapter, forming your own GROUP will go smoothly. Your GROUP will benefit the most if all members have read this book.

Before your first meeting, there are a few steps to take:

1. Determine who will join your GROUP
2. Decide the size of your GROUP
3. Choose the location
4. Familiarize yourself with this book
5. Prepare for your first meeting

1. Determine who will join your GROUP

Keep in mind that you will be sharing personal thoughts, stories and experiences so you want members who will respect the underlying purpose and trust of The GROUP. Choose people who will be mutually respectful and caring towards each other.

As communication plays an essential role in the success of your meetings, choose people who possess or are willing to develop the qualities listed in Chapter 3, *Creating The Ideal GROUP Atmosphere*, and Chapter 4, *Active Listening: The Key to Understanding Others*. The people who will create the strongest and most beneficial groups are those who are patient, open, supportive, and understanding.

Members of an effective GROUP can:
- Commit to meeting regularly
- Show up on time
- Trust and be trustworthy
- Share their feelings with others
- Practice active listening
- Accept help and insights from others

- Be mindful of the need to be right, the need to have all the "best" answers, and the need to have the last word
- Respect others' views even if they disagree with those views
- Focus on possibilities and ideas, rather than barriers or problems
- Listen without judgment
- Avoid blaming and criticizing
- Encourage others
- Think positively

2. Decide the size of your GROUP

We recommend your GROUP consist of four to six people. Should you decide to include more than six people, it would be helpful to start with a smaller group first, get your format down, and then build from there. It is fine to start your GROUP with two or three people. The number of people will determine the length and structure of your meetings.

3. Choose the location

We recommend meeting in a quiet environment where there will be no distractions. Ensure you will not be interrupted by anyone during your meetings. Your meeting space should be an environment where all members feel comfortable sharing personal thoughts and feelings. The location can vary if desired.

4. Familiarize yourself with this book

Before the first meeting, all members should read this book thoroughly. Each member should have his or her own copy to use as a handbook.

5. Prepare for your first meeting

Your GROUP should meet before your first meeting to:

- Develop your GROUP's Purpose
- Discuss and review Chapter 5, *The Structure of The GROUP Meeting*, and Chapter 6, *The Roles of The GROUP Meeting*
- Decide your meeting schedule
- Choose roles for your first meeting

Develop your GROUP's Purpose

Your Purpose is a written statement that reflects the intention of your GROUP. At the first meeting discuss what you want and expect from The GROUP. Use this time to brainstorm what you hope to see come about from your meetings. All members can share what they hope to experience as a result of the meetings. Input from everyone is important.

Once this has been discussed, combine these thoughts into a Purpose statement. Have a member type the Purpose and bring a copy for everyone to the next meeting.

Your Purpose is read by the Guide at the beginning of each meeting.

Ideas for your Purpose:

_____

_____

_____

_____

_____

The following is our Purpose:

To be or become whatever we desire.

To encourage each other to dream and inspire each other to action.

To turn possibility into reality.

The realm of dreams and imagination has no limits, so we should place no limits on ourselves.

No goal is too small or too large towards which to aspire.

We join together as a group to grow, explore and change ourselves. As we change ourselves, we positively affect our families, our communities and the world.

The power of The GROUP helps us accomplish our individual and collective goals.

To respect the trust created within The GROUP — everything we share amongst ourselves is safe and private.

This is an example of a Purpose from another GROUP:

To share, dream and create in a safe and loving environment.

To be able to communicate openly. Everything we have to say and to share is okay.

To accept ourselves and each other — unconditionally. We are allowed to be who we are.

To be part of a team; creating a foundation of support for each other on which to build. With this support a sacred space is created and there are no limits to what we can have, be, and do.

To remember that magic and miracles are everywhere — opportunities and possibilities are always present — we can help each other find them.

To discover within ourselves our own direction, guidance, and purpose.

To intentionally live our lives, with freedom and confidence.

To access the peace and the joy that resides within each of us.

Discuss and review Chapter 5, *The Structure of The GROUP Meeting,* and Chapter 6, *The Roles of The GROUP Meeting*

Discuss the five segments of a meeting. Familiarize yourself with the segments and what occurs during each of them.

Verify that the roles are understood. Review what each role entails so that everyone knows what is expected when fulfilling each role.

Decide your meeting schedule

Decide the length of your meetings and how often you will meet. We recommend a two hour meeting once a month. People tend to be busy so the meetings should be "do-able" for everyone. Time between meetings gives members the opportunity to process what was discussed and take steps towards accomplishing their goals.

An example of a 2 hour meeting is provided below:

Opening: 15 minutes
Gratitude: 15 minutes
Successes: 15 minutes
Honoring: 60 minutes
    One person is honored.
Closing: 15 minutes

If you decide to have a larger group (more than six people), you may opt to have a 2½ hour meeting with two people being honored at 45 minutes each. See Chapter 5, *The Structure of The GROUP Meeting*, for complete details.

An example of a 2½ hour meeting:

Opening: 15 minutes
Gratitude: 15 minutes
Successes: 15 minutes
Honoring: 90 minutes
    One person is honored for 45 minutes, followed by the next person honored for 45 minutes.
Closing: 15 minutes

Choose roles for your first meeting

Familiarize yourself with the roles and discuss any questions you may have. For details regarding each role, see Chapter 6, *The Roles of The GROUP Meeting*. A brief outline is provided below:

Guide

Directs the meeting, reads the Purpose and brings an Offering

Timer

Keeps track of the time during each segment, so as to keep the meeting on schedule

Honored One

Shares a goal, desired change or challenge and receives the focus of The GROUP

Action Step Writer (ASW)

Writes notes, ideas, and action steps in the Honored One's notebook as the honoring takes place

How to Form The GROUP

Decide who will be the Honored One at the next meeting. Place numbers or names in a hat and pull them to see who goes first, second, third, and so forth.

Your GROUP's honoring order:

1. _____
2. _____
3. _____
4. _____
5. _____
6. _____

This rotation stays consistent throughout all of your meetings. When you complete the cycle and everyone has been honored, start at the beginning again. The other roles (Guide, Timer, ASW) do not have to rotate in a uniform manner. After the Closing of each meeting, decide the roles for the next meeting.

When adding a new member to your GROUP, simply add him or her to the end of the rotation. This allows the new member to become familiar with the process and comfortable with The GROUP before being honored.

First Meeting

Date: _____

Time: _____

Location: _____

Length of Meeting: _____

Guide: _____

Timer: _____

Honored One: _____

Action Step Writer (ASW): _____

What to Bring to All Meetings

- An open mind
- A notebook that will only be used at your meetings
- A pen or pencil
- Excitement
- Flexibility
- Your dreams

Our Purpose

8
Permission to Dream

Time is one of the greatest factors in preventing people from following their dreams. It is easy to put off today what you can do tomorrow and before you know it, days, weeks, and even years have passed by.

You may have resistance to attending a meeting that focuses on your dreams when work is demanding, the laundry has piled up and your to-do list seems endless. Justifying precious time away from daily life—your career, your family, your home—for the purpose of attending a regular meeting can seem difficult.

You may find yourself using excuses such as:

> *"I'm too busy. I don't have time."*
> *"I'll do it when the kids are older."*

"Work is too demanding."
"My life is too crazy right now."

Excuses may always exist which means you may never find the optimal time to start or join The GROUP.

First and foremost, it is important for you to give yourself permission to dream. When you follow your dreams and take action, the empowerment you experience helps you manage life more effectively and with more enjoyment. The intrinsic value that you gain from your meetings far exceeds the actual time you spend at your meetings.

When you are part of The GROUP you become more efficient, better at communicating, stronger, and happier. Excuses do not have the power they once had. You plow right through them. Ask those who have participated in The GROUP and they will tell you that it is an experience you do not want to postpone.

> "You are the gardener of your own being,
> the seed of your destiny."
> —THE FINDHORN COMMUNITY

9
Living Your Dreams

We experience a deep sense of satisfaction when we find ways to improve our lives and become happier. When we contribute to the happiness and improvement of others' lives, this satisfaction is also felt. Being part of The GROUP accomplishes both.

You will benefit in ways you never thought possible. You will grow to believe in yourself and in others more deeply. You will move past obstacles and fears. You will accomplish goals that were, before The GROUP, only dreams.

Taken alone, the sun's rays are strong, but if one were to harness the sun's energy and focus it on an object, it becomes so powerful that it starts a fire. Herein lies the power behind The GROUP: the strength of combined energy. When you join together with others who support you, believe in you, and want to help you, what you can accomplish increases exponentially. You are empowered to achieve success and happiness in your life.

Take the steps to form your own GROUP. Make a commitment to yourself and your GROUP members, meet regularly, and watch your lives change. Make your dreams become reality.

Wishing you and your GROUP great success!

Our Offerings from The GROUP Meetings

The following are Offerings that we brought to our meetings. We hope these Offerings inspire you the way they have inspired us.

> *"If you can imagine it,*
> *you can achieve it.*
> *If you can dream it,*
> *you can become it."*
>
> –William Arthur Ward

"As a single footstep will not make a path on the earth, so a single thought will not make a pathway in the mind.

To make a deep physical path, we walk again and again.

To make a deep mental path, we must think over and over the kind of thoughts we wish to dominate our lives."

–Henry David Thoreau

"It is not the critic who counts; not the man who points out how the strong man stumbles, or where the doer of deeds could have done them better. The credit belongs to the man who is actually in the arena, whose face is marred by dust and sweat and blood; who strives valiantly; who errs, and comes short again and again, because there is no effort without error and shortcoming; but who actually strives to do the deeds; who knows the great enthusiasms, the great devotions; who spends himself in a worthy cause; who at the best knows in the end the triumph of high achievement, and who at the worst, if he fails, at least fails while daring greatly, so that his place shall never be with those cold and timid souls who know neither victory or defeat."

– Theodore Roosevelt

"And the day came when the risk to remain tight in a bud was more painful than the risk it took to blossom."

– Anais Nin

Our Offerings from The GROUP Meetings

A beggar had been sitting by the side of the road for over thirty years. One day a stranger walked by. "Spare some change?" mumbled the beggar, mechanically holding out his old baseball cap. "I have nothing to give you," said the stranger. Then the stranger asked: "What's that you are sitting on?" "Nothing," replied the beggar. "Just an old box. I have been sitting on it for as long as I can remember." "Ever looked inside"? asked the stranger. "No," said the beggar. "What's the point?" There's nothing in there." "Have a look inside," insisted the stranger. The beggar managed to pry open the lid. With astonishment, disbelief, and elation, he saw that the box was filled with gold.

I am that stranger who has nothing to give you and who is telling you to look inside. Not inside any box, as in the parable, but somewhere even closer: inside yourself.

Those who have not found their true wealth, which is the radiant joy of Being and the deep, unshakable peace that comes with it, are beggars, even if they have great material wealth. They are looking for scraps of pleasure or fulfillment, for validation, security, or love, while they have a treasure within that not only includes all those things but is infinitely greater than anything the world can offer.[3]

–Eckhart Tolle
The Power of Now

"I am much more than I think I am.
I can be much more even than that.
I can influence my environment. The people.
I can influence space itself.
I can influence the future.
I am responsible for all those things.
I and the surround are not separate.
They're part of one.
I'm connected to it all.
I'm not alone."

–William Tiller, Ph.D.
What The Bleep Do We Know!?

"Through the power of our ideas we create our world."

–David Baird
A Thousand Paths of Creativity

Our Offerings from The GROUP Meetings   161

Cliff Young

Every year, Australia hosts an 875-kilometer endurance race from Sydney to Melbourne — considered to be the world's longest and toughest ultra-marathon. The race takes five days to complete and is normally only attempted by world-class athletes who train specially for the event. These athletes are typically less than 30 years old and backed by large companies such as Nike.

In 1983, a man named Cliff Young showed up at the start of this race. Cliff was 61 years old and wore overalls and work boots. To everyone's shock, as Cliff walked up to the table to take his number, it became obvious that he was going to run. He was going to join a group of 150 world-class athletes and run! During that time, these runners didn't know another surprising fact — his only trainer was his 81-year-old mother, Neville Wran.

The press and other athletes became curious and questioned Cliff. They told him, "You're crazy, there's no way you can finish this race." To which he replied, "Yes I can. See, I grew up on a farm where we couldn't afford horses or tractors, and the whole time I was growing up, whenever the storms would roll in, I'd have to go out and round up the sheep. We had 2,000 sheep on 2,000 acres. Sometimes I would have to run those sheep for two or three days. It took a long time, but I'd always catch them. I believe I can run this race."

When the race started, the pros quickly left Cliff behind. The crowds and television audience were entertained because Cliff didn't even run properly; he appeared to shuffle. Many even feared for the old farmer's safety.

The Tortoise and the Hare

All of the professional athletes knew that it took about 5 days to finish the race. In order to compete, one had to run about 18 hours a day and sleep the remaining 6 hours. The thing is, Cliff Young didn't know that.

When the morning of the second day came, everyone was in for another surprise. Not only was Cliff still in the race, he had continued jogging all night.

Our Offerings from The GROUP Meetings   163

Eventually Cliff was asked about his tactics for the rest of the race. To everyone's disbelief, he claimed he would run straight through to the finish without sleeping.

Cliff kept running. Each night he came a little closer to the leading pack. By the final night, he had surpassed all of the young, world-class athletes. He was the first competitor to cross the finish line and he set a new course record. He finished the race in 5 days, 15 hours and 4 minutes. Not knowing that he was supposed to sleep during the race, he said when running throughout the race he imagined that he was chasing sheep and trying to outrun a storm.

When Cliff was awarded the winning prize of $10,000, he said he didn't know there was a prize and insisted that he did not enter for the money. He ended up giving all of his winnings to several other runners, an act that endeared him to all of Australia.[4]

Notes

[1] This chapter adapted from Rebecca Carswell's book, *Hey, Are You Listening to Me? Listening Your Way to Professional and Personal Success*, with permission.

[2] Author Unknown. Story printed on a variety of websites. Story originally received via email.

[3] Reprinted with permission from *The Power of Now*, 1997, New World Library, Novato, CA. www.newworldlibrary.com.

[4] Various sources available: http://en.wikipedia.org/wiki/Cliff_Young_(athelete) and http://www.elitefeet.com/the-legend-of-cliff-young-the-61-year-old-farmer-that-won-the-worlds-toughest-race.

Author Biographies

Rebecca Carswell

Originally from New Hampshire where she attained her Bachelor of Science degree in Marketing, Rebecca Carswell moved to Florida in 1998 to pursue her enjoyment of skydiving. It was through skydiving that she met her husband, Mike. In 2002, Rebecca broke her back in a skydiving accident. Despite a negative prognosis from doctors, Rebecca recovered completely and the injury became a turning point in her life. The experience led her to become a clinical hypnotherapist, study the world's religions for two years, and become a spiritual counselor. Rebecca is also a professional speaker. Her topics include improving communication skills and dealing with negativity in the workplace. She currently lives in Florida with her husband and their four cats.

Mirja Heide

Born in Denmark, Mirja Heide moved to Florida when she was eight years old. She earned a Bachelor of Science degree in International Business with a certification in Environmental Studies from Florida Atlantic University. Since graduating, Mirja has been an entrepreneur. She first started an international trading company which focused on African markets. A few years later, she coupled her extensive computer experience with an interest in working with people to start a computer training and consulting company. Mirja is celebrating 10 years of a successful business and enjoys the role of translator, bridging the gap between people and technology. She currently lives in Florida and enjoys photography, kayaking, yoga and traveling.

Tiffany Kaharick

Originally from Pennsylvania, Tiffany Kaharick grew up in Florida. With a Bachelor of Science degree in Cardiopulmonary Science, Tiffany enjoyed an exciting career as a Respiratory Therapist in Orlando, Florida, where she was a member of a medical helicopter team. In 1999, she began skydiving as a hobby. She is currently a licensed massage therapist, living in Florida with her fiancé, Ian. Writing a book fulfills one of her lifelong dreams.

Amy Mead

Amy Mead is originally from Chicago, Illinois. Since the age of five she has enjoyed horseback riding, which contributed to her great appreciation of the outdoors. Amy received a Bachelor of Fine Arts degree from Connecticut College and then worked in the graphic design business in Chicago for 12 years. In 2001, Amy and her boyfriend, Cameron, moved to Florida and bought a 27-foot sailboat. For one year they lived aboard their boat, exploring the east coast of Florida and the islands of the Bahamas. Upon their return, Amy started her own advertising company. She currently lives in Florida with Cameron and their daughter.

To Reach the Authors

Website:
www.TheGroupTheBook.com

General Information:
info@TheGroupTheBook.com

To Reach the Authors:

Rebecca Carswell: rebecca@TheGroupTheBook.com
Mirja Heide: mirja@TheGroupTheBook.com
Tiffany Kaharick: tiffany@TheGroupTheBook.com
Amy Mead: amy@TheGroupTheBook.com

PRESS

www.FocusOnEthics.com